History of the World

The Salem Witch Trials

Stephen Currie

KIDHAVEN PRESS

THOMSON
™
GALE

Detroit • New York • San Diego • San Francisco
Boston • New Haven, Conn. • Waterville, Maine
London • Munich

Library of Congress Cataloging-in-Publication Data

Currie, Stephen, 1960–
  The Salem witch trials / by Stephen Currie.
    p. cm. — (History of the world)
    ISBN 0-7377-1038-1 (hardback : alk. paper)
    1. Trials (Witchcraft)—Massachusetts—Salem—Juvenile
literature. 2. Witchcraft—Massachusetts—Salem—History—
17th century—Juvenile literature. 3. Salem (Mass.)—Social
conditions—Juvenile literature. [1. Trials (Witchcraft)—
Massachusetts—Salem. 2. Witchcraft—Massachusetts—Salem.
3. Salem (Mass.)—History—Colonial period, ca. 1600–1775.]
I. Title. II. Series.
  KFM2478.8.W5 C87 2002
  345.744'50288—dc21

2001006123

Contents

Introduction

Early in 1692, a terrible scare swept through Salem, Massachusetts. The troubles began when several young girls accused three townspeople of using witchcraft. As time went on, the girls **accused** more and more people. By the late spring, more than one hundred people had been named as witches.

The adults of the town were surprised by the accusations but took them very seriously. Almost all of the people who had been accused of witchcraft were charged and put on trial.

These trials are known today as the Salem Witch Trials. The trials were a sad time in American history. The people who had been accused said they were innocent, but they could not get the judges to believe them. One by one they went to trial, and one by one they were found guilty. By the time the scare died down later that fall, about twenty people had been put to death for being witches.

The trials were not a complete shock. Most people in Massachusetts at the time believed in witches. They thought that the devil used witches to spread evil. When bad things happened, they believed witches had caused the problem. Other Massachusetts towns had witch trials, too.

A witness testifies at a witch trial in Salem, Massachusetts.

Massachusetts: Scene of the Salem Witch Trials

But none of these towns had trials that were quite like Salem's. In most of these other towns, only a few people were accused of witchcraft. When they were put to death, the scare was over. No one knows exactly why Salem was different. No one knows today why the scare in Salem was so big, or why so many people were named, or even why so many adults believed the accusations. All anyone knows is that it *did* happen that way—and that the time of the Salem Witch Trials was a sad and scary time.

Chapter One

The Witch Scare Begins

During the winter of 1692, strange occurrences began happening to nine-year-old Betty Parris and her cousin Abigail Williams, two years older. The girls, who both lived in Betty's house, suddenly began spending most of their time curled up in corners, ignoring everyone around them. From time to time they shrieked as if they were in pain, although no one was touching them. Their bodies twitched and twisted into awkward positions.

Betty's father, Samuel, was the minister of Salem Village's **Puritan** church. When the behavior did not stop after a few days, Samuel and his wife called in a doctor. The doctor could find no physical explanation for the fits. Another doctor was called in, but he also found nothing.

Meanwhile, girls who were friends with Betty and Abigail started to have the same kinds of fits. Twelve-year-old Ann Putnam was affected. So was sixteen-

An actress plays Abigail Williams, who seemed to be under the spell of witchcraft.

year-old Mary Walcott, and a twenty-year-old servant girl named Mary Warren. Soon, about a dozen girls in Salem were acting like Samuel's daughter and niece.

Finally, Samuel Parris called in a new doctor, William Griggs. Griggs examined Betty and Abigail carefully. At last he said that he had figured out the problem. At first he had thought it was a physical disease, he said, but it was not. Instead, it was witchcraft. The girls were under a spell.

Who?

The Puritan Church offered several cures for people who had been bewitched, including prayer and fasting, or not eating for a time. Over the next few weeks, the people of Salem did both. Still, the girls did not get better. If anything, their twitching and screams became more violent.

By the middle of February, many of the villagers were growing nervous. They believed that some evil townspeople were working with the devil to bewitch

A Puritan man prays for an afflicted girl to be delivered from a witch's spell.

the girls. They insisted that the girls tell who was causing their fits. Samuel Parris joined them in demanding names. Finally, at the end of the month, the girls began to accuse people.

The first person they named was Tituba Indian, a slave who lived in the Parris household. Samuel Parris believed the girls. So did most of the other villagers. Still, they doubted that Tituba was the only witch. They asked the girls if there were others. This time the girls named two more women of the village: Sarah Good and Sarah Osborne.

Tituba was a slave, part black and part Native American. In both ways, she was very different from the other people of the town. Sarah Good and Sarah Osborne seemed different, too. Neither woman attended church, during a time and in a place where nearly everyone went. Sarah Good was a poor beggar, known around the village for muttering to herself. Sarah Osborne had married her servant after her first husband's death—a decision that shocked the townspeople.

"Why Do You Hurt These Children?"

On February 29, 1692, the three women were arrested. The next day all were brought to the church, where they were questioned by village officials called **magistrates**. The questioning was called a **hearing**. Its purpose was to decide if the three women should be brought to trial.

An actress plays Tituba Indian, the first person in Salem accused of witchcraft.

Sarah Good was questioned first. She insisted she was innocent, but the magistrates treated her harshly. "Why do you hurt these children?" they asked, as if they had already found her guilty. "I do not hurt them," she said. "I scorn it."[1]

But few people believed her. To the magistrates and the villagers, the **evidence** against Sarah Good seemed very strong. Her mumblings might be curses, people thought. Worse, her own husband testified that Sarah was probably a witch. Even Sarah's four-year-old daughter, Dorcas, said that she had seen her mother send three birds to torment the girls.

Still, the worst testimony came from the accusers. The chief magistrate asked the girls if Sarah had done them harm. The girls said that she had. Then they fell into fits. When they had recovered, they said that Sarah's spirit had done the dirty work.

Sarah Osborne was next. Like Sarah Good, she insisted that she was not a witch and said that she had not caused the girls' problems. If the girls had seen her, she said, it was only the devil in disguise. "I do not know the Devil," she argued. "I never did see him."[2] As with Sarah Good, however, the magistrates did not believe her.

Tituba's Testimony

Tituba's testimony came last, and it was the most dramatic of all. Like Sarah Good and Sarah Osborne, Tituba said at first that she had never hurt the girls. But as the questioning went on, the slave woman began to change her story. Although she had not wanted to harm the girls, Tituba explained, she had no choice. "The Devil came to me and bid me serve him,"[3] she said.

As the magistrates listened, Tituba described her dealings with the devil. He had come to her several times, she said, promising her presents if she did what he wanted. The devil had brought along Sarah Good and Sarah Osborne, too, and three other witches—two women and a man whose names she did not know. Tituba explained that the devil had made her spirit join them in hurting the children.

Tituba's testimony was very important. As the magistrates saw it, her words proved that the devil was involved. Her testimony also seemed to show that all three women were guilty. Tituba confessed and accused the other two as well.

But most important, Tituba's statement suggested that the girls were right all along. The accused women *had* been visited by evil spirits, and the evil spirits belonged to the women they had accused. The

A film scene shows Tituba and village girls gathered around a bubbling cauldron.

This magistrate and his colleagues accept the stories told by the girls as proof that the accused are witches.

magistrates decided that the girls' word was all the proof they needed. The women could deny that they were witches, but they could not change the minds of the officials.

Over the next few days, the magistrates questioned Tituba, Sarah Good, and Sarah Osborne again. But Good and Osborne now had no way to defend themselves against the charges. Even if they could prove that their bodies had been somewhere else, the girls could still say that the spirits of the accused had tormented them. As everyone expected, the magistrates decided that the girls were right. On March 7 the three women were thrown into jail. The next step would be to bring them to trial.

Chapter Two

More Accusations

With the three women in jail, most people in Salem expected that the excitement would calm down. But it did not. The girls were still suffering from fits. According to Tituba, three more witches existed, and the magistrates decided to find them. During the next few days they asked the girls to tell them more about the spirits who were tormenting them.

Martha Corey

They did not have to ask many times. On March 11, Ann Putnam accused Martha Corey of being a witch. At first, no one wanted to believe that Corey could be a witch. Unlike Sarah Good, Sarah Osborne, and Tituba Indian, Martha Corey was an important and hardworking member of the community who always attended church. Many people in Salem liked and admired her.

Still, Ann Putnam did not stop accusing her. A few days later, Abigail Williams also called her a witch. At first, Corey had not been afraid of the accusations. But she soon began to worry. Later that day, she went to Ann Putnam's house. She wanted to tell Ann that she was not trying to hurt her in any way.

But Corey never got the chance. The moment she stepped into the house, Ann started to have a terrible attack. First she began to choke. Then she said she could not see. Although it was hard for her to talk, she accused Corey again of being a witch. She also said she had seen Corey's spirit beating her family's servant girl, Mercy Lewis. Suddenly, Mercy began to twitch and choke, too.

An Arrest

The Putnam family ordered Corey to leave. They were convinced that she was bewitching the girls. That Sunday, the girls interrupted the church service many times with their fits. At one point, Abigail Williams shouted that she could see Corey's spirit on the ceiling. That was enough for the magistrates. They arrested Corey and brought her in for questioning.

Corey's hearing was very much like the earlier ones. "I am an innocent person," she told the court. She said that she was no witch, but a "Gospel woman,"[4] a Christian who loved and feared God. But every time she spoke or moved, the accusers in the audience screamed or twisted in pain. They said

Abigail Williams, played by an actress, accuses Martha Corey of witchcraft.

The unfortunate Martha Corey stands trial for witchcraft.

Corey's spirit was pinching and biting them. The magistrates sent Martha Corey to jail.

Power

By now, other people in Salem were saying witches had cast spells on them, too. Some of these accusers were elderly women. A few others were men. Sometimes they added evidence against the women whom the girls had already accused. Ann Putnam's mother, for instance, told the court that Martha

Corey's spirit had come to her. As she put it, the spirit was "ready to tear me all to pieces."[5]

But the new people also made new accusations. So did the girls who had started the witch scare. Over the next three months, more than one hundred people were charged with witchcraft. Some of them were like Sarah Good and Sarah Osborne—women and men who seemed different from others in the village. But more and more often, they were not.

The magistrates were surprised to hear some of the accusations. Some of the most respected people in Salem were being called witches. Several more church members were accused. So were a few wealthy farmers. Even a minister, George Burroughs, was charged with practicing witchcraft.

A Surprise

Of all the people accused, though, probably the biggest surprise was Rebecca Nurse. She was an elderly woman who was believed to be a good Christian. Some villagers thought she was the most moral person in town. But before long Ann Putnam's mother accused Rebecca Nurse, and soon several other people agreed that she practiced witchcraft.

The magistrates had a hard time believing the charges. One even said he hoped Nurse was innocent. But they brought her in for questioning anyway. When her accusers started to twist and scream with pain, Nurse agreed that they were probably bewitched. Still, she insisted that she had not hurt anybody.

But not even Rebecca Nurse could convince the judges. The shrieks and moans of the accusers were too much for the officials. The only answer for this odd behavior seemed to be witchcraft. Because the accusers said it was Nurse's fault, she ended up in jail. So did nearly everyone else who was questioned.

John and Elizabeth Proctor

It is hard to know today why some Salem villagers were accused of being witches, while others were not. Perhaps the accusers were already angry at certain people, and used charges of witchcraft to get back at them. Perhaps the girls and the other affected adults were just naming any names they could think of. No one knows for sure.

Historians *do* know, however, that it was foolish to disagree with the accusers. People who tried to stand up to them were often called witches themselves. That was especially clear in the case of John Proctor.

John and his wife Elizabeth Proctor owned a large farm and a tavern. They were church members and well liked in the village. From the beginning, John Proctor spoke out against the witch craze. He said that the girls were making it all up. He even threatened to beat his servant, Mary Warren, if she did not stop having fits. Very soon, Mary's attacks stopped.

The other girls, however, quickly accused both Proctors of witchcraft. The Proctors said they were innocent. But when the girls screamed through their hearings, the magistrates sent both Proctors to jail.

An actor portrays John Proctor, who argued that claims of witchcraft were untrue.

The young accusers inspired fear among the townspeople.

Later, the girls also accused Mary Warren and three of the Proctors' children of witchcraft.

John Proctor was probably not the only villager who believed the girls were lying. But when other people saw what happened to him, they decided to keep their doubts to themselves. It was too dangerous to disagree with the girls and the other accusers. They had become the most powerful people in Massachusetts.

Chapter Three

The Trials

By early June, the trials were ready to start. The Massachusetts governor named several important judges to be in charge of the trials. The judges chose a **jury** of men who lived in Salem. The jurors would decide whether the accused people really were witches. If the people were found guilty of witchcraft, then the judges would decide on a sentence, or punishment.

The judges also thought about the question of proof. What kind of evidence would prove that a person was really a witch? The judges came up with a list. If people admitted to being witches, for example, then they could be found guilty. They could also be found guilty if they were accused by a witch who had already confessed. That had happened during the hearings, when Tituba named Sarah Good and Sarah Osborne as fellow witches.

The judges had other ways of proving that a person was a witch, too. For instance, people at the time believed that witches could not say the Lord's Prayer. The judges decided that they would find people guilty of witchcraft if they made mistakes while saying the prayer.

The judges also agreed to use something called a touch test as evidence. In this test, the judges waited until an accuser was having a fit. Then they forced the

Actors portray the stern magistrates in charge of the witchcraft trials.

accused witch to touch the person who made the accusation. If the fit stopped, it proved that the accused witch was guilty.

Finally, the judges had to decide what to do about the accusers' stories of being attacked by spirits. The magistrates accepted this kind of proof, which was called **spectral** evidence. The magistrates believed everything the girls said, no matter how bizarre it seemed. The judges decided to do the same. One single accusation would be enough to find a person guilty. There was very little hope for the prisoners now.

The Trials Begin

The trials began in early June. The first person to be tried was a Salem woman named Bridget Bishop. The judge and the jury began by hearing from several witnesses who had known Bishop for many years. These witnesses said that they believed she was a witch for a long time. One man said he was sure that Bishop had bewitched a pig that he kept on his farm. Two workers said they had been in her house, where they had seen puppets stuck with sharp pins. Many people believed that was a sign of witchcraft.

Next, the judges heard from people who said that Bishop had tormented them. Abigail Williams spoke at this time. So did Ann Putnam. Mary Warren said that Bishop's spirit was still attacking her, even from jail. Bishop had a turn to defend herself. When the judges asked if she was a witch, she said very firmly

A hysterical Mary Warren (front) claims that Bridget Bishop cast spells on her even from jail.

that she was innocent. But the girls sat in the courtroom, screaming and thrashing with pain when she spoke. The jury quickly decided that Bridget Bishop was guilty.

At this pace, it seemed that the trials would move along quickly. Then one judge, Nathaniel Saltonstall, told the others that he thought the trials were unfair. He said that spectral evidence was not really proof. He also thought the accusers should not be allowed in the courtroom when they were having fits. When the other judges refused to change their rules, he quit the court in protest.

Some of the girls were furious at Saltonstall. They accused him of witchcraft. But this time they went too far. Another judge talked sternly to them. Saltonstall was *not* a witch, he said, and they should not make accusations about such an important person. The girls quickly took back what they said.

More Trials

The trials went on and another judge replaced Saltonstall. The new trials were very much like Bridget Bishop's. The judges and jury sat at the front of the room facing the audience. The prisoners and witnesses were called one by one to the front. The judges asked questions, and the prisoners and the witnesses answered. The room was filled with villagers, including the accusers, who sat up front and often fell into fits.

The judges usually began by hearing from people who had known the accused for a long time. Often they heard that the person on trial had threatened someone, or might have used witchcraft to make someone ill. Then the judges heard from the accusers. Under questioning, the accusers described exactly how the accused witch had tormented them. And they continued to have fits in the front rows.

There was no defense against this spectral evidence. Sarah Good was tried and found guilty. So was Martha Corey. So were John and Elizabeth Proctor.

The tormented faces of John and Elizabeth Proctor. Both were found guilty of witchcraft.

The minister George Burroughs argued that witches did not exist, but the jurors did not believe him. They found him guilty, too.

Rebecca Nurse

When Rebecca Nurse came to trial, though, the mood changed. The accusers said again that Nurse's spirit had tormented them. But many of Nurse's friends and relatives told the court that the stories could not possibly be true. They talked about her good deeds and her kindness. The jurors listened carefully and found her not guilty.

Rebecca Nurse was free—or was she? The moment the jurors gave their verdict, some of the girls in the audience fell onto the floor in terrible fits. They cried that Nurse's spirit was trying to kill them. The head judge was worried. He thought they were telling the truth, so he asked the jurors to think again. Maybe Nurse was guilty after all.

The jurors were not sure what to do. Finally, one of them asked Nurse a question about something she had said earlier. Nurse did not reply. Probably she did not hear him; she was old and growing deaf. But now the jury was taking no chances. They changed their minds: Rebecca Nurse, they said, was guilty of being a witch.

Sentences

The penalty for witchcraft was quite serious. All the people who were found guilty were sentenced to death by hanging. The first to die was Bridget Bishop on June 10. Others soon followed. By the end of September, nineteen convicted witches had been hanged.

The hangings were public: The judges invited the townspeople to come and watch, and many did. The judges also let the accused witches speak to the crowd. Some, like John Proctor, were badly frightened. They begged to be allowed to live. But others, like Sarah Good, were angry. "I am no more a witch than you are a wizard,"[6] she told a man who was there.

George Burroughs tried to prove that he was no witch, and it almost worked. Just before he was hanged, he said the Lord's Prayer without making a

Those found guilty of witchcraft, including John Proctor (center), were carted off to be hanged.

George Burroughs, shown during his arrest, nearly escaped the gallows by reciting the Lord's Prayer perfectly.

single mistake. The people were amazed. After all, everybody thought that witches could not say the Lord's Prayer. Burroughs had done it, so he could not be a witch. A few men began to talk of setting Burroughs free.

But a Boston minister stepped forward. "The Devil has often been transformed into an angel of light,"[7] he told the crowd. His meaning was clear. The devil told Burroughs what to say. Burroughs might sound like a godly person, but he was still a witch.

The men moved back. The hanging took place as planned. A few minutes later George Burroughs was dead.

Chapter Four

The Scare Ends

During the summer of 1692, more than twenty-five people were found guilty of witchcraft. Most of them were put to death right away. But a few were not. Elizabeth Proctor was pregnant, and the judges decided to wait until after she had given birth. Another woman escaped from jail before she could be hanged.

Four other women avoided death by confessing. The judges said they would spare the life of anyone who admitted being a witch, as long as that person seemed truly sorry. The four women had to stay in jail, and they had to give up their property to the government. But they were not put to death.

By now, many prisoners were choosing to confess before they came to trial. After all, the jury did not believe any of the accused witches. Some of the prisoners decided that staying alive was more important than trying to convince the jurors that they were innocent. So they admitted they were witches as soon as they were put in jail.

The prisoners' confessions were often bizarre. They told about secret meetings at night with the

Elizabeth Proctor was pregnant when she was found guilty of witchcraft.

devil. They described how they flew above the trees on sticks and poles. Some said they had been witches for years. Those who claimed to be witches were lying, and they knew it. But as one group of prisoners put it, "There was no other way to save our lives."[8]

Giles Corey

A few of the accused witches were tortured into confessing. One of these people was Giles Corey, the husband of Martha Corey. Giles Corey refused to say anything at all about the accusations against him. He would not say he was a witch. But he would not say he was innocent, either.

Giles Corey had a good reason for saying nothing. If he confessed that he was a witch, he would lose his

Some of the accused confessed to bizarre behavior like riding sticks in the sky.

property. But if he said he was innocent, then he would be put on trial and probably be found guilty. Either way, he knew that the government would take his property.

There was one way out: keeping silent. According to the law, people who refused to talk could not be put on trial. As long as Giles Corey said nothing, he could keep his property away from the government and pass it down to his children.

It was a dangerous plan. The judges were eager to bring Giles to trial, so they decided to torture him. They made him lie on the floor, placed a board across his chest, and put heavy rocks on the board. Soon the weight began to crush his chest.

The judges thought that Giles would want to stop the pain. When it got heavy enough, they said, he would either agree to a trial or confess to being a witch. But they were wrong. Giles Corey chose to die under the board. His body was crushed. But his property went to his children as he wished.

Changes

Even during the trials, the accusations did not stop. All summer long, the girls kept having fits. Sometimes they blamed the attacks on people already in jail. But often they accused new people. These people were arrested, and the jails filled.

In July, there was a witch scare in Andover, a nearby town. The minister there invited Ann Putnam and Mary Walcott to help find the witches in the

The girls who made the first accusations continued to have fits during the course of the trials.

town. The girls used the touch test to see who was guilty. In all, they accused sixty-seven people of witchcraft. Those people were sent to jail. Some came to trial in Salem.

But by September, some of the villagers were getting a little tired of all the accusations. They remembered George Burroughs saying the Lord's Prayer, and they wondered if he really had been a witch. They remembered how John Proctor had been arrested because he questioned whether the fits were real. They remembered Rebecca Nurse and her kindness.

Now, too, the girls were accusing very important people. They accused some of the governor's advisers. They accused two rich merchants. They accused the wife of Increase Mather, a Boston minister. Not even the judges could believe that all these people were guilty.

By October, a lot of people were unhappy about the way the trials were being handled. Increase Mather wrote a long letter to the judges. He agreed that *some* of the prisoners might have been witches. But he also said that some innocent people had been hanged.

Witch-Hunt Victims

People	Salem	Andover
Accused of witchcraft	100 +	67
Hanged	19	3
Pressed to death under a board heaped with rocks	1	0
Died in prison	4	1

Mather thought that this was not a fair trade. It would be better, he said, "that ten suspected witches should escape, than that one innocent person should be condemned."[9]

Mather suggested making an important change. He said that the court should not use spectral evidence any more. Nor should it use the touch test, or ask people to say the Lord's Prayer. Many other ministers agreed. So did some government leaders.

Freedom

In late October, Governor William Phips of Massachusetts formed a new court to hear the rest of the witch cases. This court did not allow spectral evidence, touch tests, or the Lord's Prayer. Instead, the judges would look for witnesses who had seen the accused people practicing witchcraft. If there were no witnesses, then the prisoners would be found not guilty.

This time, nearly all the prisoners were found not guilty. The judges did sentence three people to death, but Phips overturned their sentences. By this time, the people who had confessed were asking to take back their confessions. They said they had been so frightened that they had lied. Phips agreed. By April 1693, all the accused witches were out of jail.

For a while, the girls kept making accusations. But no one took them seriously. As people stopped listening to them, they stopped having so many fits. Slowly, their lives returned to normal.

Massachusetts governor William Phips formed a new court that was to rely only on the testimony of eyewitnesses.

The freed prisoners did their best to get back to normal, too. But for most of them, life would never be the same. Elizabeth Proctor, for instance, had a new baby—and no husband. Many of the accused witches came home to find their farms a tangle of weeds. A few of them lost all their land and belongings while they waited for their trials.

Anger and Apologies

The angriest people, though, were the friends and families of the people who had been put to death. They were sad and furious that their loved ones would be remembered as witches. Some of the fami-

An actor portrays a magistrate. Some judges felt that the first court in the witch trials used faulty procedures.

lies asked officials to admit they had been wrong. But the officials would not admit it.

Soon, though, that began to change. Some of the people involved in the trials wondered if the trials were fair. Samuel Parris, the village minister, supported the witch-hunt from the start. But in 1694 he told members of his church, "I may have been mistaken."[10]

Parris was only the first. Two years later, one of the judges said he was ashamed of what he did. Over the next few years, so did some of the jurors. Finally, in 1706, Ann Putnam spoke up. She had accused many people of being witches. Now she said she was very sorry for her actions. "I have . . . good reason to believe they were innocent persons,"[11] she admitted.

Forgiveness

By now, most officials had changed their minds. In 1711 a court ruled that the accused witches were innocent. The court also paid back the victims for the property they had lost. The village church forgave its members who had been accused. Some had been dead for nearly twenty years. Still, most people agreed that showing forgiveness was the right thing to do.

Although the witch craze is long over, the trials are still remembered. They are an example of what can happen when people are too quick to make accusations, and not careful enough to protect each other's rights.

Notes

Chapter One: The Witch Scare Begins

1. Quoted in Richard B. Trask, *The Devil Hath Been Raised*. West Kennebunkport, ME: Phoenix, 1992, p. 5.
2. Quoted in Trask, *The Devil Hath Been Raised*, p. 8.
3. Quoted in Trask, *The Devil Hath Been Raised*, p. 10.

Chapter Two: More Accusations

4. Quoted in Trask, *The Devil Hath Been Raised*, p. 39
5. Quoted in Trask, *The Devil Hath Been Raised*, p. 33.

Chapter Three: The Trials

6. Quoted in Larry Gragg, *The Salem Witch Crisis*. New York: Praeger, 1992, p. 155.
7. Quoted in Chadwick Hansen, *Witchcraft at Salem*. New York: George Brazillier, 1969, p. 148.

Chapter Four: The Scare Ends

8. Quoted in Gragg, *The Salem Witch Crisis*, p. 133.
9. Quoted in Gragg, *The Salem Witch Crisis*, p. 175.
10. Quoted in Gragg, *The Salem Witch Crisis*, p. 184.
11. Quoted in Gragg, *The Salem Witch Crisis*, p. 187.

Glossary

accuse: To say that a person is guilty of a crime or an action.

evidence: Proof, especially in a court case.

hearing: A court proceeding to decide if a person should be brought to trial.

jury: A group of citizens who decide if a person is guilty of a crime.

magistrate: A court official who can act as a judge.

Puritan: A Christian church common in New England in colonial times, or a member of that church.

spectral: Having to do with spirits.

For Further Exploration

Dorothy and Thomas Hoobler, *Priscilla Foster: The Story of a Salem Girl*. Parsippany, NJ: Silver Burdett Press, 1997. A fictionalized account of the witch scare.

Stuart A. Kallen, *The Salem Witch Trials*. San Diego: Lucent Books, 1999. Describes the trials and puts them in their historical context.

Zachary Kent, *The Story of the Salem Witch Trials*. Chicago: Childrens Press, 1986. How the witch scare began and how it ended.

Stephen Krensky, *Witch Hunt*. New York: Random House, 1989. A short account intended especially for young readers.

Earle Rice Jr., *The Salem Witch Trials*. San Diego: Lucent Books, 1997. Part of the Famous Trials series.

Lori Lee Wilson, *The Salem Witch Trials*. Minneapolis: Lerner, 1997. Gives information about what historians think about the witch-hunt and describing the trials. Also talks about modern-day "witch-hunts."

Index

Picture Credits

About the Author

Stephen Currie is the author of more than forty books, including a number of works on history and some historical fiction. He is also a teacher. He grew up in Illinois and now lives with his family in upstate New York.